holy dreams
to feed the soul

a book of prayers and meditations by
Garth Hewitt

photographs by
Wilf Whitty

for Aisha Grace,

Caitlin Faith

and Siyanda Sandino

First published in Great Britain in 2007

Society for Promoting Christian Knowledge
36 Causton Street
London SW1P 4ST

British Library Cataloguing-in-Publication Data
A catalogue record for this book is available from the British Library

ISBN 978—0—281—05964—5

1 3 5 7 9 10 8 6 4 2

Designed and typeset by Theresa Maynard
Printed in China by 1010 Printing International Ltd

contents

preface

I was very glad to be asked to do a follow-up to *Making Holy Dreams Come True*. I had very much enjoyed working with Wilf on that book: I love his photos and we have had the opportunity to travel together again since then to South Africa, and to stroll together round the East End of London. This book contains morning and evening daily prayers as before and then two other chapters.

Chapter 2, 'Deserts and healing fountains', is a response to our world and a search for a spirituality to help us move forward in times like these. It also contains a section of prayers related to a difficult time of illness; my youngest son had a series of operations and a long time in hospital. Many families have to go through such stressful times and, like my own family, may have found it to be a wilderness time spiritually. I hope expressing my feelings may be a help to others.

The final chapter, 'Prayers around the world and prayers for pilgrims', once again visits parts of the world where Amos Trust has partners — in particular Nicaragua and South Africa — but also focuses on the area where I live in the East End of London, which I find to be a fascinating area and a place of great refreshment.

To find out more about Amos Trust projects, visit our website at www.amostrust.org or contact us at Amos Trust, All Hallows on the Wall, 83 London Wall, London EC2M 5ND; phone: 020 7588 2661.

As before, some of these prayers have been tried out in the liturgies for Wednesdays on the Wall, held at All Hallows on the Wall in the City of London.

For more information on these services, go to www.allhallowsonthewall.org.

Although the prayers and meditations are primarily for personal use, some are suitable for use in communal worship. Archbishop Tutu said, 'God has a dream', and gave us a wonderful vision of that dream. I hope that these prayers, meditations and photos will sharpen our 'holy dreams' by giving us a better understanding and enjoyment of God's dream for us all.

Garth Hewitt

E ORIGINAL

ALL GOLD

NO PRESERVATIVES, COLOURANTS OR THICKENER

"Appetite's Temptation"

chapter 1

---

daily prayers

sunday morning

O God, thank you for this day
It is the pause that restores
A day of hope — a day to breathe
The day of resurrection
A day of restoration.

May I take time to give thanks today
And stop and think today
And show love today
And look around and enjoy the world today
And take time with you today
And so find renewed strength today
O God, thank you for this day.

sunday evening

God made known in stillness
I love the quiet of Sunday evenings
Getting ready for the week
In this moment of stillness —
Maybe stillness before tomorrow's storm.
When I was a child we sang evening hymns
Strangely comforting songs like
'The day thou gavest, Lord, is ended
The evening falls at thy behest.'
It gave a sense of order
Rather like a benediction
You have given the day . . . and now
You bring the night for our rest.
As I place family, friends and loved ones into your hands
I want to thank you for this day
I close my eyes, put myself in your hands
And look forward to tomorrow.

monday morning

O God, give us the courage for today's tasks
There may be difficult decisions
It may be a day or even a week that will be very busy
Despite that, may I take time to pause and laugh
And relax even in the busy moments
To walk humbly with you
God of the ordinary and the remarkable
God beside us
God with sleeves rolled up
God in the noise and rush
Yet God most clearly in the pause, the stillness
And the deep, deep silence.

monday evening

God of the darkness
God of the evening star
I place myself into your hands this night.
As I lie down to sleep
I ask for a quiet mind
And a still spirit
I ask for forgiveness
And the refreshment of your spirit
And remembering you are also God of the light
And God of the morning star
I place tomorrow and all its many activities
Into your hands.
May I not worry in advance
But sleep in peace.
Good night.

tuesday morning

Lord, I am lost without you
I cannot enjoy life without you
You give me my meaning — my way to live
You transform my mind
So I do not conform
You show me what is good — what is acceptable
You call us to love — to hold fast to the good
To be honourable — and dignified
To always maintain hope
To be patient in the hard times
To care for others
To delight in other people's moments of joy
And empathize in their struggles
To live in harmony — and care for those that society
    values the least
And to live peaceably . . . and never take revenge
To overcome evil with good . . . and never take revenge.

Thank you, God, for all the tasks we have to do
And for giving us a spring in our step
And renewing our vision
And for walking beside us.

tuesday evening

God of the just heart
In the challenging words of the Sermon on the Mount —
'Blessed are those who hunger and thirst for justice
They shall be satisfied' —
You remind us that satisfaction does not lie where we
    might expect it —
In the security of wealth and privilege —
But in the joy of doing what is right
And in working to assert the value and dignity of
    other people
Because this is the calling of your community
This builds relationships and just societies
This brings deep satisfaction
As all are made welcome.

So keep us hungering and thirsting
For the values that make us all whole
And then we know the healing fountains will start.

wednesday morning

God of the passionate heart
Thank you for the values of your alternative community
They give us vocation
They show us causes
They show us the value of our neighbours
How to love one another
Why one person being treated unjustly matters
Because you are the God of the passionate heart
You are the God committed to the poor
We are in a world where they are forgotten as the rich
    get richer
You are the God who calls for purity of heart
You are the God who calls for action
For us to do justice and show mercy and walk humbly —
Thank you for the values of your alternative community
They give us our passion for life.
May we never lose our sense of calling.

wednesday evening

O God, the words of Jesus —
'Blessed are the peacemakers' —
Resonate from Matthew's Gospel reminding us that
'They will be called the children of God.'
What higher ambition!
In Luke's Gospel we find the same theme
As Jesus calls us to
'Do good to those who hate you'
To bless, love, do good, lend, give
'And you will be the children of the Most High.'
What higher calling!
How different from the messages we receive day after day
In our media and advertising
But it is the road of healing, of community.
O God, keep us conscious of that high calling
So we are called children of God.

thursday morning

Lord, in times like these how should I live?
Show me the path of peacemaking.
I bring my prejudices to you
And ask that you will continue to convert me
Day by day and step by step on the way
So that I never build up walls of division
But become one of those who show that
In Christ these divisions are finished.
Lord, may I be a child of God
Walking steadily on the path of peacemaking.
And will you feed my soul, nourish my spirit and lift me up.

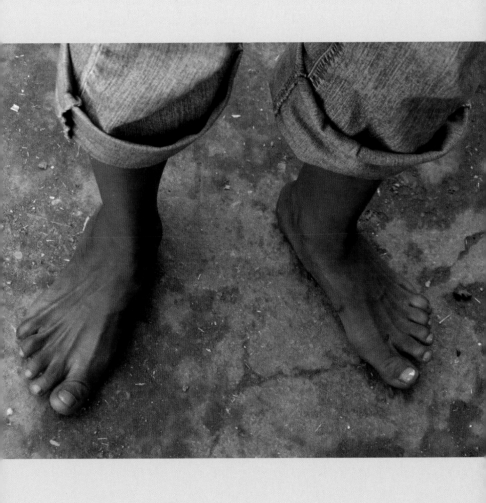

thursday evening

God, creator and sustainer
'Blessed are the meek, for they will inherit the earth.'
How these words resonate now
As the greedy consume the earth
And make it vulnerable for our children and grandchildren
But you teach us to say 'enough' and to share
And to sacrifice and to enjoy it
All because it brings life to others.
We have now agreed to spend twenty-five billion on a
    Trident nuclear submarine
Annually we spend billions on war
But the Millennium Development Goals to reduce poverty
Look even farther away.
Teach us to be the meek — and to rethink our priorities
And to treat this beautiful world with gentleness
And study war no more.

friday morning

Encouraging God, may I have your mind and your love
May I learn the humility of Jesus
Doing nothing from selfish ambition
But walking the humble way
Looking to the interests of others
Having the mind of Jesus
Who humbled himself
And walked the road of non-violence
Rejecting the ways of manipulation and domination.
Such love has inspired so many down through the centuries
May it inspire me today to show love
To be an encourager and to bring hope to others.

friday evening

God of the wise chuckle
Give me wisdom . . . and humour
Like an Archbishop Tutu —
He has wise words we need to hear
Like, 'If you are neutral in situations of injustice
You have chosen the side of the oppressor.'

So teach us to beware of the word 'balance' —
It means keeping things as they are
Preserving the status quo —
Where there is imbalance
We need to restore equality and justice.
Righteous God, stir us up
To be those who are passionate for what is right
So we do not fall into the temptations of silence, neutrality
   and balance
That see people in their suffering . . .
And simply leave them there.

saturday morning:
a thought for breakfast

In Proverbs it says that 'honey is good'
And wisdom is like 'honey to the soul'
'If you find it, you will find a future,
And your hope will not be cut off.'
Again and again it calls for wisdom and knowledge —
This is how a house is built
How rooms are filled.
As I put honey on my toast this morning
I am reminded — we need a little honey for the soul
A little taste of wisdom
We should treasure wisdom.
Lord, grant me wisdom to understand situations
And then courage to do what must be done.

Proverbs also says —
'One who gives an honest answer
Gives a kiss on the lips' —what a great thought
It makes honesty sound rather sexy
And so it should!

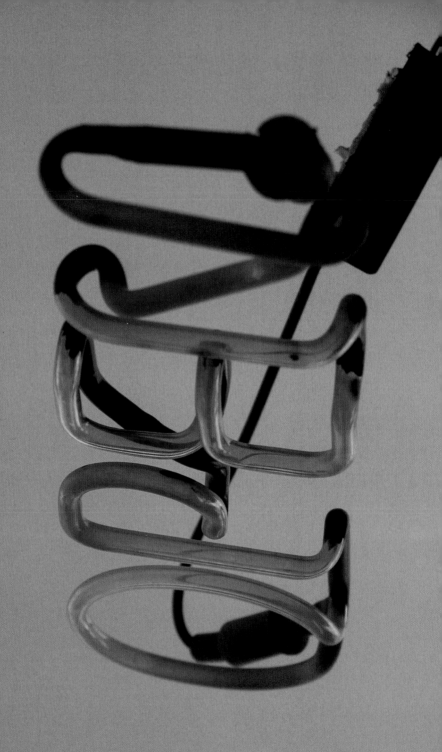

saturday evening

Ezra Pound said that 'what we love well will remain
The rest is dross'.
God, teach me to love your ways
To be pure in heart
To be committed to what matters
To be open-hearted and open-spirited
To love our sisters and brothers who are forgotten
To be sensitive to those whom life and society seem
    to push down
To love the ways of joy, peace, patience, kindness,
    generosity,
Faithfulness, gentleness, and self-control.

chapter 2

---

deserts and healing fountains

from the deserts
of the heart

W. H. Auden talked about the 'deserts of the heart'
And our hearts feel like deserts now
Dry and parched, cracked and broken.
Our dreams of yesterday are long gone — even look embarrassing
Like dancing with joy when New Labour came to power . . .

But now we are dry and our visions have shrivelled.
They shrivelled as we heard the lies that defended war —
As we destroyed with 'shock and awe' — as the death
   toll mounted —
As the torture increased — as David Kelly died —
As Jean Charles de Menezes was assassinated —
As our religious leaders kept quiet and did not march —
As our politicians competed to point fingers at our Muslim
   community
As our politicians competed to sound more extreme —
All in the name of the new god 'security'
Dancing to the dangerous rhythm of a tabloid drum
Dancing to the dangerous rhythm of the instant soundbite
Dancing to the ancient rhythm of 'empire'
As our religious leaders kept quiet and did not march . . .

How many vigils at Downing Street and rallies in Trafalgar Square
And march after march from the Embankment through Whitehall
And on to Hyde Park? And the ordinary people came . . .
Because they sensed something was wrong
They marched for humanity — they marched for peace —
They sensed the Holy Spirit . . .
So they held their banners high, they lit their candles
As our religious leaders kept quiet and did not march . . .
They were busy 'straining at gnats' and 'swallowing camels'.

healing fountains
start again

Our ability to dream was dying of thirst . . .
But even in the desert you never leave us without witnesses
And prophets did rise up like Brian Haw and Norman Kember
    and Chris Cole
And other ordinary people who marched and marched . . .
Though they were ignored . . .
And so healing fountains did start again in the deserts of
    the heart
And though the forces of militarism and domination are just
    as strong
Somehow they look more foolish now . . . because people
    questioned and marched . . .
And they still do and no one can stop them
And our world looks more fragile and vulnerable now
And we know deep in our hearts we must learn to listen —
We must learn to question — we must love our neighbour —
Or die.

And one day the mountains will be brought low and the
    valleys lifted up
The proud will be scattered and puzzled
And the powerful brought down from their thrones
And the rich will wonder at their emptiness
And the hungry will be filled with good things
Because good people did not keep quiet
When deceit and evil were flourishing . . .

And they will take the religious leaders by the hand
And help them to speak again — maybe a child will lead them —
So they rediscover their voices and learn how to march . .
And dream dreams and prophesy once again.

in the deserts of the soul

A shrivelled soul is a terrible thing —
It cannot be watered by money
It cannot be bought or fooled by a soundbite
It feels pain surrounded by luxury
Because it knows how most people are living
Not in the greed of indulgence
Or conscience-destroying wealth
But in the daily struggle for food and water
Longing for healthcare and education.
But there can be wealth of a different type
The wealth of a heart constantly open and hands open in giving.

Lord, I have just fled from Miami,
As the super-rich come in for three major boat shows,
And returned to the City of London where now you can even
    have sprinkled gold
On top of your drinks.
O Lord, I fear for the souls of the cities of wealth — and I
    pray for them.

Good Lord, deliver them from the awful burden of money
And the fearful state of an unwatered soul.
But I can point the way to a place of learning and restoring
Where I was before Miami — where hearts and hands are open.

finding tears to
water the soul

In Nicaragua — where most people do not have a job —
Most do not have enough to eat
But here your soul may find refuge and be renewed
As they show you a gospel of love that touches the
    forgotten poor
Where they will show you an open and caring community
Where people have time and creativity and love
And they believe in justice for all and in loving your neighbour.

And when I stood in their church in Managua tears flowed easily
And I felt the restoring move of the Spirit saying,
'The boat that you must row cannot carry gold
Or weapons that maim or kill, it will destroy your soul
So leave it all behind for a much, much better way.'
And I thank you, God, for words that heal —
For examples that restore —
For a place and a community
That can water the deserts of the soul.

the love of money

On reality shows and quiz shows
From City excess to casinos,
From the arms sold to war zones
As the gap between rich and poor grows
As ice-caps melt and rainforests go
As we keep control of the oil flow
Use naked power in Guantánamo
Arbitrarily bomb a new foe
Start to reap what we have sown
Because that's the way the money goes
Since the love of money as we should know

. . . is the root of all evil.

The next four meditations relate to a time of illness in the family and the struggles it brought.

falling out with god

We stopped talking, Lord.
I was used to rolling with the punches and I always sensed
    you there
Then I took the knock-out punch . . . and you stayed silent
I was brought up with Mahalia singing, 'His eye is on the sparrow
And I know he's watching me' — and then the eye was not there.

My youngest son going through operation after operation
And in the desperate pain he cried out —
In the night he cried out — and you were not there
We had told him you would be with him
Through the struggle — not to solve it
Not to take away the pain but you would be the companion
But he said, 'I cried out and no one heard me
There is nothing and no one there.'

Even that was not my final straw — something further went
    wrong and I broke
I remember the moment — in the lift —
When I said, 'You have made my life a mockery
I thought we had a deal — maybe even a covenant
But you were not there.'

So I stopped talking to you . . . for months
Two can play at silence
I walked in the desert alone — I walked the Mile End Road alone
Between home and hospital.

My Jewish friends argue with you more — I learned from them
Where were you in the valley of the shadow?
Where was the rod and staff when we needed it?

following . . .
from a distance

But I could not live with the silence
I blinked first — I gave in
I started talking to you again . . . really by habit

Now my understanding has changed for good
Now I know you as God the encompassing spirit
Not as the God who intervenes
(I journeyed from supernatural theism to panentheism
says the theologian Marcus Borg!)

Somehow in the silence — when we were not talking —
I understood and moved on
I simply cannot see life without seeing you interwoven
I could not live without praying — it is so like breathing
So I am back on 'the way' — I am following . . .
But from a distance

And way back in the further distance
I sometimes see another figure — with dark glasses on —
Walking with dignity . . . and watching . . .
Always watching
It is my son.

the christmas we
never prayed

Our custom was always to pray at our Christmas Eve meal
But one year we did not pray — actually — we could not pray
It had all been too painful
Too many operations — too much time in hospital
Too much uncertainty for the future
Too much shock — not just for us —
But friends were suffering too around the world
And especially in Palestine
Yet this was the year we needed to pray
Job did not give up when he was battered —
But we were not able to pray — we were injured.

In cricket when a batsman is injured
He has a runner — to run between the wickets
In life when we are broken — everyone needs a prayer —
Somebody who prays when we no longer can
And we were fortunate — we had a prayer
And he would phone week after week
To get his update
Then he did his task 'between the wickets' —
In the hard times everyone needs a prayer
For the times you cannot pray
And in the strong times maybe we can be the prayer for
    someone else.
We pray at other times over Christmas now
But we still cannot pray at the Christmas Eve meal . . .
But it will return
— it will return.

thanks to a friend

You always knew when to call —
In the most poignant and difficult moments you kept in touch
On the worst day of all you came
Walking into the hospital when all was crisis
And in the shock in your face I knew we had support
I knew I had a friend.
I have found it hard to tell you since
Because tears come too easily
And frankly I become incoherent
And you look puzzled and slightly worried about me!

But I thank God for you
A true friend in the hard times
Is a true friend indeed
In a dry time you brought water.
Thank you.

a little to feed the soul
(thoughts from santa's ghetto)

Each year in the run-up to Christmas a group of artists —
Including graffiti artists — open a store of creative, subversive,
Humorous, irreverent, reverent, rude and prophetic art —
It is called Santa's Ghetto.
This year it was in Oxford Street in London.
In the window was a picture by Peter Kennard
Showing Tony Blair taking a photo of himself on his
    mobile phone
Smiling and putting himself in situ with an exploding Iraq
    behind him.
This picture was having a huge impact on the street
As tourists stopped to photograph it themselves.
Inside towards the back I found a little piece by Lucy McLauchlin
It said, 'In our world today we have plenty to stimulate all
    of our senses
Yet little to feed the soul.'
And suddenly all the noise of Oxford Street disappeared
A simple truth cut through
In the busyness of all the multiple stimuli
The most liberating moment can be the moment of quiet
The moment when we realize the beauty of human values
When we discover the silence we call God
The moment where in the stillness our imagination is liberated
In the silence encounter begins
In the silence there is a still small voice
We meet ourselves and we meet God
But unless we pause we can find our soul remains unfed.

we are accepted

Welcoming God, refresh our view of you
And our understanding of you
May we remember that in you and with you there are no strangers
With you we are accepted
You are truly the God of love
Keep opening our eyes to see this truth
May we walk away from excluding others from you and your love
And from fullness of life
May we never lose the simple faith
Of knowing we can make a difference
If we accept others as you accept us.

chapter 3

---

prayers around the world and prayers for pilgrims

a prayer from iraq

(Based on a photo in the *Guardian* on 12 March 2007)

Loving God, the destruction and suffering of Iraq is quite
   overwhelming
Where do we start to pray — can we ever see a glimpse of hope?
Picture after picture of bomb damage . . .
And then there it was — a poet standing in the rubble
Reciting one of his poems
I nearly wept — Ahmed Abdel Sara was standing in the ruins
   of al-Mutanabi street in Baghdad
A few days earlier a bomb hit the street and thirty were killed.
Now we learn that many Iraqi poets have taken to reciting
   their poems
Among 'the charred manuscripts and destroyed buildings'
Of this area famed for its booksellers.

And people are sitting round listening
Some holding books or pieces of paper
This is a picture I shall remember —
Here is a glimpse of the spirit of the people unbowed and creative —
Refusing to give in despite the brutality and violence visited
   upon them.

So, Lord, we pray for Iraq — for its poets and writers
Hope bringers and dream weavers —
Thank you for their courage.
We long to see peace amidst this awful destruction
The powerful came with 'shock and awe'
And bombed relentlessly and rained destruction
Now a poet stands and recites his words
Like a seed of hope longing to be watered.
O God, send the rain — this time healing rain
That will bring restoration to this wonderful old country.

nicaragua pilgrimage:
nicaragua is holding its breath

A spark of hope is lit again in Nicaragua
A new president — a new morning
But can he deliver?
So many hungry, so many poor
But at least a new president that says he is for the poor.
Expectations are raised — but even water is scarce
In the first month the President brings in free schooling
And free health care and cuts his salary in half
The community are almost holding their breath with hope.
God of the just heart, we pray for Nicaragua
Thank you for these glimmers of optimism
May the spark of hope become a fire of joyful reality.

poetry in granada

As we drive into Granada —
There is a banner across the road saying —
'Poetry is a human right'.
Where else in the world I wonder would you be greeted like this?
O God, my heart is regularly thrilled in Nicaragua by such
    incidents
Such a creative land of art, culture, music, architecture
And of course poetry . . . and in so many ways the spirit is fed.

They have just had a poetry festival that included 'poetry walks'.
They would walk together around the town and then at
    certain points
They would stop and a poet would read a poem.
The most famous poet of Nicaragua, Ruben Dario, lived
    here briefly
 (though his home, now a museum, is in Leon)
 So did Ernesto Cardenal, priest, social activist and author
    of many books of poetry
Including the epic poem — 'The Cosmic Canticle'.
When he became Minister of Culture
In the previous Sandinista government in 1979
He gave his family home to the municipality as a cultural centre —
Now a school for music, painting and dance — an inspiring
    place to visit.
Creative God, thank you for all that inspires the imagination
In the beautiful land of Nicaragua.

a visit to old leon

This is the place of the first cathedral in Nicaragua
Called St Mary of Grace
And a monastery here is called the 'Monastery of Mercy'
But here there was no sign of grace or mercy
By the ruins of the monastery our guide pointed out
That churches were a way of oppressing —

Nearby was a hall called 'the hall of shouting' —
Thousands of slaves were taken here to be branded —
Later to be sold to Panama.
They found gold in Old Leon and the Spanish took this.
A striking statue remembers the fate of the local people —
If they disobeyed the Government they were thrown to
    trained killer dogs.
On the place of the statue sixteen native Indian chiefs were killed.

After we heard all of this we walked up a hill
And stood looking over the lake at two volcanoes
Momotombo and the smaller one Momotombito
This is truly a land of lakes and volcanoes.
As we drove away from Old Leon
We drove through a more modern small town —
Ironically it is called Peace Town.
Peace, mercy and grace seemed absent when Church and Bible
    were used to oppress
Yet this strikingly beautiful land has gone on to struggle for
    liberation
Liberation of land, liberation of people, and even liberation
    of religion.
May we carry on the task of liberating religion
From its temptation to dominate and oppress
And keep learning from history
And God of mercy, grace and peace, may we never again
    hide your image
And your ways.

the cross of spain in rivas

La Cruz d'Espania is the place of the first meeting in Nicaragua
Between the Spaniards and the native Indians.
It took place in 1521 and was a philosophical discussion between
Chief Nicaro, who was questioning
The leader of the Spanish expedition — Gil Gonzalez.
Chief Nicaro asked many questions —
'Have Christians news of the great flood that flooded the earth . . .
And will there be another one?'
'When would the sun and moon lose their brightness?'
'Why are stars so big and who holds them?'
'Where are the souls of bad people?'
'Where do souls go after death?'
'Will the Pope ever die?'
'Is God a human?'
'Why do so few people want so much gold?'
And so it went on — history suggests that after hearing
   Gil Gonzalez's answers
He accepted Catholicism . . . but did he . . . ?
There was also a rumour that suggested that he may not
   have done.

But we can learn from Chief Nicaro's style of questioning —
Maybe this is the way we should question our leaders
A few key theological points and then —
'When will this beautiful earth be destroyed?' and
'Why do so few people want so much oil?' and so on . . .
The symbol of the cross at Rivas is painful for Christians
It symbolizes a faith brought with violence, brutality and torture
Yet it can also teach us to keep on questioning.

an east end pilgrimage:
an early spring day in
st katharine's dock

Thank you, God, for a walk by St Katharine's Dock
It is the beginning of February but it feels like a spring day
Boats are moving from basin to basin
Tourists are strolling enjoying the sun
Here in the shadow of history — by the Tower of London —
Is a place to relax and my heart is full
And I thank you, God,
For beauty seen in this place and in the people walking by
And even in the humour —
Today the wonderful old statue of Trajan at Tower Hill
Has a cigarette dangling from his bottom lip — it looks hysterical!
It reminds me that just down the road in a small dank back alley
Leading to the River Thames, in the least prepossessing
   spot on earth
The graffiti artist Banksy has stencilled
OFFICIAL DESIGNATED PICNIC AREA
Thank you for little glimpses of humour that send us on our
   way chuckling . . .
Especially on the bonus of an early spring day.

christmas eve in the tower

What a beautiful yet ambivalent evening in St Peter ad Vincula —
A lovely chapel in the heart of the Tower of London — lit only by
    candlelight
A wonderful choir sings the carols that have been sung through
    the years
The service, in the language of 1662,
Must have been said here most Christmas Eves since then.
Here we celebrate the birth of the Prince of Peace
Over a place where fifteen hundred bodies were buried
Thirty-three are now buried beneath the altar — some
    famous names like
Anne Boleyn, Lady Jane Grey or Catherine Howard,
The Duke of Monmouth, who led a rebellion;
There is also a memorial to the Duke of Wellington who brought
    victory in war.
The chaplain talks of Bethlehem and talks of his experiences in
    the Middle East.
I am grateful because I had been to another carol service
That entirely ignored the current situation in Bethlehem.
So I pray for my friends in Bethlehem — surrounded by a wall
As tonight I am surrounded by a wall
And I pray for peace in a place that reverberates with memories of
    blood and vengeance
And I pray about the news today in a place resonant with history
And I pray for healing in the Holy Land in a place
Where in earlier times people would have set out on crusades

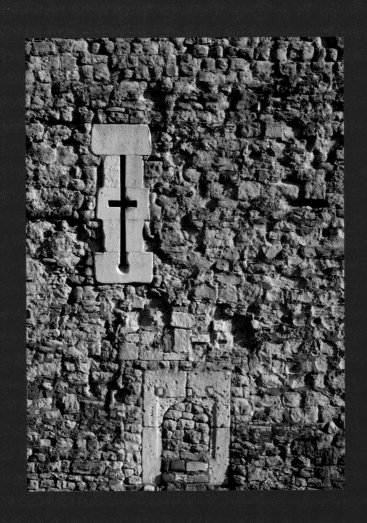

And I long to feel hope in my soul . . .
But I feel fear for the citizens of the 'little town'
Cut off, surrounded and under siege in Palestine.
I think of the wonderful, hopeful birth of the baby . . .
   but I also think of Herod
And I shiver . . .

brick lane

Beautiful streets like Fournier Street and Princelet Street
Run from Spitalfields Market to Brick Lane.
These are the houses of the Huguenots who fled to Britain
   from France
To avoid religious persecution after the massacre of
   St Bartholomew's Day in 1572.
There is a building here that tells a story and sums up the
   history of the area —
It is on the corner of Fournier Street and Brick Lane.
It was built first as a chapel for the Huguenots — L'Eglise Neuve
Later it became the Spitalfields Great Synagogue
and now it is the Jamme Masjid Mosque.
It reflects the different immigrant groups that have come
   to this area —
Found a home — then gradually moved on.
It reflects the desire to worship in different yet similar ways.
It reminds us of the contribution that each group brings.
No. 19 Princelet Street has even become a museum to refugees.
God of the alien and the stranger, teach us to value the
   contribution of all
Especially those coming to our country as refugees or
   asylum seekers.

by the waters of wapping

We should all have a place of peace
A place to stroll and think and pray
And mine is Wapping where I live
I am so grateful, Lord, for this beautiful and fascinating place.
Thank you for walks by the River Thames
There is always something new happening
Even if I did miss the whale . . .

From the pier-head to the Prospect of Whitby
I walk and study the local history
Then on to Limehouse and down to Canary Wharf
With pubs en route all apparently once frequented by Charles
    Dickens and Samuel Pepys
The painter Turner came down to Wapping —
Living here for short periods under another name —
Lord, I am grateful for the fascinating stories.
The *Bounty* and the *Endeavour* both left from Wapping
Captain Bligh lived here and Captain Cook up on the Mile
    End Road
Hymn writer James Edmeston was born in Wapping —
    he wrote the hymn
'Lead us, heavenly Father, lead us o'er the world's
    tempestuous sea'
John Newton lived here — slaver who turned to Christianity and
    wrote 'Amazing grace'.
Sadly slaves must have walked these streets
The Museum of Docklands tells us all about this aspect of the history

Also more light-hearted recent history —
The Beatles were photographed on the pier-head
The day before recording 'Hey Jude' —
So much history — so many stories
But in the evening walking by the river after a busy day I find
    I am restored
By the waters of Wapping I pause, think and pray and meet
    you there.

at the crossroads:
a prayer for the holy land
in holy week

Merciful God, we remember the forgotten faithful
Of the Holy Land during this holy season.

Despised and rejected they, like all Palestinians,
Are living at the crossroads — one way leads to hope —
The other to despair. Many are leaving — they can take it no longer —
Denied their democratic rights they feel betrayed by
   talk of peace

That has only brought more checkpoints, more closures
    and curfews,
More land taken and a huge separation wall that imprisons them
And strangles their economy.
We pray that the deep suffering of occupation will cease.
May we ignore them no longer — after forty long years
In this wilderness of despair may the world say 'enough'
And walk with them towards a promised land of hope and dignity.

Israelis also live at the crossroads —
Carrying the scars of centuries of suffering —
May they find liberation from their fears and a way to walk forward
May international law be honoured — so both Israeli and Palestinian
Can live in peace — both live securely — both live in freedom
Without walls and occupation and fear.
May Muslim, Christian and Jew find a way to live together
So this land once called 'holy' becomes holy again —
So Jerusalem becomes a holy city again
'Where all who will may enter and no one is denied'
And may we play our part by making sure
That we hold all communities in our hearts.

hidden from view

Wounded God — why do we dislike some people so much
That we build walls around them and hide them from view?
Is it fear that drives this strange paranoia?
People should not be hidden from view —
Our giving should be and even our praying —
But not people — they are treasure.
We are building more walls now —
Especially to hide Arabs in Palestine and Iraq.

The remarkable theologian Bishop Kenneth Cragg says,
'Only wounded hands can reshape the world.'
And he points out that following God's example
There is no place now
For the law of revenge in God's community
This vulnerable God does not resort to any strategy
Where the other is denied or coerced
Or hidden from view.

durban south africa pilgrimage:
a morning walk in durban

God our constant companion, we took a walk today
On the streets of Durban — we met many street children
Nxampofu on crutches — his joints going because of sniffing glue
Bheki — his arm broken and leg damaged after being hit by a car
He could not afford any medical treatment
So Umthombo's 'Street Team' were hoping to help him
Mbali and Smanga — brother and sister living just off Point Road
The most dangerous place to be
They have lost both parents — and have no family left.
We were taken around by members of the Durban Street Team
    including
Osaviour and Nokukhanya — both had previously been
    on the streets
And had lived in one of the most notorious shelters on the
    Point Road

We also met a policeman who came to warn us
That it was dangerous for tourists to be with these young people
He yelled at them to get back — we would be robbed
He said, 'We can't solve the problem so we contain it.'
I told him we worked with Umthombo to help the children
And he shook my hand and thanked me.

But I worried about just 'containing' the problem
There is a better way that would be better for all the community —
To take them off the street.
Umthombo took three hundred and twenty-five children off the
    street last year
And already sixty-two this year.
One week later Osaviour came to see me thrilled with excitement
The Street Team had managed to get Mbali and Smanga
To a place of safety run by the municipality.
God, who walks beside us on our encounters —
Strengthen the Durban Street Team in this work that restores
    hope and dignity
To the most vulnerable young people.

a holy moment in durban

It looked like a Eucharist . . .
Of bread and soda drinks
We were in a little lock-up or shed — once perhaps a garage
Here around twelve to fifteen street children huddled
The smell of urine hit you powerfully when you walked in
This was a Dickensian scene of life at its hardest
The shelter even had a lethal-looking power box
With the electricity still working — the children played
   with the wires —
One had received a shock
Bizarrely there was even a double bed and a headboard.
We heard stories of children thrown out of shelters and homes
Like Bianca who had been in the lock-up for a month
After being thrown out of a shelter when she had had a baby.
She said, 'The white people chased me away.'
They say she cannot support her daughter.
They have even kept her daughter but will not let her visit.
She is seventeen and has been on the streets from 1999.
When she was chased away from the shelter
This group of street children welcomed her and said,
   'Come and stay.'

But then the Street Team brought sodas, fruit juice and bread
And the children queued to receive
One of the elder street children distributed
He happened to be wearing a cross

It looked like a Eucharist
And in the deepest sense I knew it was.
Children deserted by the world
Let down by those they should trust
Given a holy meal and this was the real presence of God
Seen in Umthombo's Durban Street Team
As they counselled and organized hospital visits for those
    who were sick
And listened to their stories and needs
It was a holy moment in such a broken place

now I am only
fighting with my pen

O God, thank you that Thabisile is back at school
May this be the start of a new life for her.
Thabisile Shandu came on the streets in 2002 —
She was thirteen. Her mother died in that year —
    an AIDS-related death.
She went to stay with her older brother
But as she put it, 'He slept with me so I decided to run.'
On the street she was often on glue — 'It stopped me feeling cold
    and hunger.'
On being asked how she survived on the street
She said, 'The street taught me how to fight.'
She survived by petty stealing — but now she is back at school
    life has changed
She says, 'Now I am only fighting with my pen.'

Thabisile lived with many other street children under a tree in
    an area called Parkview.
Umthombo's Durban Street Team have given her the opportunity
    to go back to school —
They have supported her to make it possible.
She says, 'I am happy now — even proud of myself.'
She wants to be a social worker — 'I would like to help other
    street kids
So they don't have to sleep on the roads like us.
I would like them to have a better life than me.

At school her favourite subject is English — she is very articulate
and can write well.
O God, thank you that Thabisile is back at school — thank you
for her talents
Bless her and give her the strength to continue
So she can realize her ambitions and be a blessing to others.

benedicite

(after visiting umfolozi game reserve and st lucia
wetlands heritage site)

O African lion, leopards and cheetahs, praise the Lord
Remarkable giraffes hiding behind trees, praise the Lord
Impala, nyala, eland and kudu, praise the Lord
Praise God, whose love endures for ever.

Grey heron flying down the estuary, praise the Lord
Great egret and secretary bird, praise the Lord
Crocodiles lazing in the sun
And powerful hippos with their young, praise the Lord
Praise God, whose love endures for ever.

Black rhinos and white rhinos, buffalo and wildebeest,
    praise the Lord
Romantic zebra, bushbuck and steenbok, praise the Lord
Male rogue African elephant chasing us down the road . . . please
    stop — and praise the Lord
Praise God, whose love endures for ever.

Warthog and mongoose, hyena and vervet monkeys, praise
    the Lord
Samango monkeys and strange-bottomed baboons, praise
    the Lord
Golden-tailed woodpecker, grey go-away-bird and African
    crowned eagle, praise the Lord
Praise God, whose love endures for ever.

God in creation — God of evolution
God of great trees and myriads of plants
God of birds and animals — some curiously strange
God interwoven, God ever moving, always inspiring and
    bursting with hope
Putting our lives into perspective — taking our breath away
God of the great African sky — of the wide and vast
    African landscape
We praise you — whose love endures for ever.

a sword will pierce your own heart

The healer brought pain
The one with the easy yoke brought turmoil
Just as Mary's soul was pierced
With the death of her son
So our hearts are pierced
By the death of so many
And God's heart is pierced
By the oppressed and forgotten
And Mary feels the pain of her dying son
And God feels the pain of the dying children
A sword of betrayal pierces the Holy Land
A sword of prejudice rejects people —
People, Lord, that you call holy —
Because all are holy in your eyes —
And our hearts are pierced as our friends suffer
As our friends are betrayed at the hands of the powerful
At the hands of the dominant and rich
And our hearts are pierced by the sword of injustice
Like the spear that pierced the side of Jesus
We cry out in pain for our wounded friends
Our prayers are not heard — the Church remains silent
The western world supports the wielding of the sword
The vulnerable are struck down
Why — why is there no healing?
A sword pierces my heart . . .
I am wounded deep.

easter

Holy Week is a breathless journey that turns our world upside down
Then Easter comes in like a tornado of hope and revolution
From Palm Sunday the alternative procession has started —
Not the procession of empire and power
That would have been the way the Romans marched into Jerusalem
But the procession of freedom, liberation and non-violence
As Jesus came into Jerusalem — gentle and riding on a donkey.
A week later it leads to the encounter on the Emmaus road
Where we meet him in the breaking of bread
Where we realize that Jesus,
Killed by the authorities on Good Friday,
Is vindicated by God on Easter Sunday —
Jesus is Lord — not the powers of the world.

This is the way — the way of the community of God:
Alternative, subversive, hopeful, full of laughter, joy and freedom —
On a donkey — affirming people's value and dignity
It all bursts forth at Easter — the way of Jesus is vindicated
And so filled with this spirit — bursting with renewed hope —
We set off to live 'the way' of good news and liberation.

Thank you, risen Jesus, that you go before us
To the Galilee of ordinary everyday life
Where we are called to live this alternative and liberating way.

photographs